EQUIPPING THE SAINTS

BOOK 1 EVANGELISM MINISTRY

YINKA OLOYEDE

GLORY PUBLISHERS AND RESOURCE SERVICES

EQUIPPING THE SAINTS

BOOK 1 EVANGELISM MINISTRY

We are All called to Evangelise, but some have been gifted to Evangelise as Traveling Missionaries.

2 Timothy 4:5, Amplified Bible

… do the work of an evangelist, fully perform all the duties of your ministry.

Ephesians 4:11, Amplified Bible

11 And His gifts were [varied; He Himself appointed and gave men to us] some to be apostles (special messengers), some prophets (inspired preachers and expounders), some evangelists (preachers of the Gospel, traveling missionaries), some pastors (shepherds of His flock) and teachers.

Table of Contents

DEDICATION 5

INTRODUCTION 6

CHAPTER 1 11
   Equipping the Saints ....

CHAPTER 2...20
   Living in A Dying World..

CHAPTER 3...28
   Evangelism Made Simple..

CHAPTER 4 36
   Evangelism as a Personal Witness of the Christian Faith .

CHAPTER 5...56
   Be Equipped to Be Sent Out ....

ABOUT THE AUTHOR 71

DEDICATION

I dedicate this handbook, to Jesus Christ, my Lord and Saviour who died for my sins, so that I may receive forgiveness and live a life of abundance.

I desire to serve Him to the Best of my Revelation of knowing who He is to me

INTRODUCTION

When we look at the body of Christ at large, we have become so comfortable in our nice-looking Churches either the small or huge ones. We spend so much money on making the place look so beautiful and comfortable that we forget it is just a building where we meet as a local body. We are comfortable in our church buildings than going out to BE the Church. We are the Church; we are the spiritual Church or the real Church because we carry the spirit of God in us. We bring life to the building when we come together in our local churches. Jesus told His disciples to go out into all the world and preach the Gospel. In the book of Revelation 14:14, talks about the harvest is ripe - the harvest for the souls of men needs to be harvested before the coming of our Lord Jesus Christ. Now is the time for us to leave our beautiful Churches, Evangelise and bring in the harvest.

Evangelism is also a way to bring the body of Christ together in a community, as we jointly come together for soul winning. Evangelism is a way of expressing love to those who do not know Christ and their lives are full of crisis and issues, The hopeless; and the atheists who are ignorant or deny the fact the God even exists. Through Evangelism, we can win them into God's Kingdom.

Equipping the saints is a book series which will comprise of the five-fold ministry gifts, which are the Apostles, Prophets, Pastors, Teachers and

Evangelist. Each book will be written in a simple, practical way for a better understanding of each ministry gift and how each gift functions.

BOOK 1 EVANGELISM MINISTRY is the first book in this series. If we can all have a better understanding about evangelism, we can all evangelise in one way or the other, either as individuals, a local church or churches coming together.

Many people are shy to go out and evangelise because they do not know how to approach a person or what scriptures to use, this book explains simple ways to approach people in different categories and scriptures to back you up.

As the body of our Lord Jesus Christ, after reading this handbook, we have no more excuses for not witnessing to others.

Church leaders, Ministry leaders, Ministers in different areas or believers in a small group or large, make *this book a Must read* for all the people around you.

I pray that this book will evoke the body of Christ to be uncomfortable in our nice-looking churches but go into our communities and preach the Gospel and know that Evangelism is a MUST for all believers.

Our Lord Jesus Christ is soon to come, therefore let us strive to win more souls into the Kingdom before He comes.

In His Service

Yinka Oloyede.

CHAPTER 1

Equipping the Saints

Equipping the Saints Series is for those who want to become mature saints and leaders in the body of Christ.

The first step to becoming a leader in the body of Christ is to fully understand what Apostle's Paul message was then and still now, to the saints in Ephesians chapter 4. Once you have a revelation or insight about this chapter, you have laid a foundation for yourself of what it means to be a real saint or a minister in the body of Christ.

As a believer, it is crucial you live a Christ-like life; this is who you became when you decided to follow Him, let people see His Light shine through you.

All believers are ONE regardless of our denominations, ministries, House of prayers etc. We have only One Label:

We are the body of Christ, and He is the Head of His Body, which is the Church.

Therefore, we must live in Unity of our Faith in Christ.

Christ knew before time, that to become like Him and for His body to be One, we would need to be divinely educated. For this reason, He gave some according to the grace He bestowed upon them, the grace to be Apostles, Prophets, Evangelists, Pastors and Teachers. We need all these gifts to become full matured saints in the body of Christ. Every sector of the body of Christ needs all. One cannot do without the other because they all have a specific function in perfecting the saints.

Christ knew before time that in the last days, many would be deceived for lack of sound doctrine. In the church today, we have many ungodly teachings or doctrines such as Deceptive doctrines, Gambling doctrines, Lying doctrines, Witchcraft doctrines and doctrines of demons; all for the intention to lure the saints into confusion. These kinds of doctrines have caused deception and disunity amongst the saints so they cannot attain the full stature of Christ. Once the body is disunited, and each believer does not understand who he or she is in Christ, we become immature saints and leaders, and hence, we don't have what it will take to be the Glorious Church that Christ is coming for when He returns.

THE EQUIPPING OF THE SAINTS SERIES is for every believer and leader in the body of Christ. As the body of Christ, it is crucial for us to understand our role as saints and ministers. When we do have explicit knowledge about who we are and our roles, then we can further understand that we only become perfect when we walk in unity with all parts in the proper places and playing their unique role. At that point, we build a full mature church in the body of Christ, which will shine her Glory prepared for the day of the coming of Christ.

Read the Bible passage with an open mind considering what I have just explained.

Ephesians 4:1 – 16, Amplified Bible (AMP)

I, therefore, the prisoner for the Lord, appeal to and beg you to walk (lead a life) worthy of the [divine] calling to which you have been called [with behaviour that is a credit to the summons to God's service,

2 Living as becomes you] with complete lowliness of mind (humility) and meekness (unselfishness, gentleness, mildness), with patience, bearing with one another and making allowances because you love one another.

3 Be eager and strive earnestly to guard and keep the harmony and oneness of [and produced by] the Spirit in the binding power of peace.

4 [There is] one body and one Spirit — just as there is also one hope [that belongs] to the calling you received —

5 [There is] one Lord, one faith, one baptism,

6 One God and Father of [us] all, Who is above all [Sovereign over all], pervading all and [living] in [us] all.

7 Yet grace (God's unmerited favor) was given to each of us individually [not indiscriminately, but in different ways] in proportion to the measure of Christ's [rich and bounteous] gift.

8 Therefore it is said, When He ascended on high, He led captivity captive [He led a train of [a]vanquished foes] and He bestowed gifts on men.

9 [But He ascended?] Now what can this, He ascended, mean but that He had previously descended from [the heights of] heaven into [the depths], the lower parts of the earth?

10 He Who descended is the [very] same as He Who also has ascended high above all the heavens, that He [His presence] might fill all things (the whole universe, from the lowest to the highest).

11 And His gifts were [varied; He Himself appointed and gave men to us] some to be apostles (special messengers), some prophets (inspired preachers and expounders), some evangelists (preachers of the Gospel, traveling missionaries), some pastors (shepherds of His flock) and teachers.

12 His intention was the perfecting and the full equipping of the saints (His consecrated people), [that

they should do] the work of ministering toward building up Christ's body (the Church),

13 *[That it might develop] until we all attain oneness in the faith and in the comprehension of the [[b]full and accurate] knowledge of the Son of God, that [we might arrive] at really mature manhood (the completeness of personality which is nothing less than the standard height of Christ's own perfection), the measure of the stature of the fullness of the Christ and the completeness found in Him.*

14 *So then, we may no longer be children, tossed [like ships] to and fro between chance gusts of teaching and wavering with every changing wind of doctrine, [the prey of] the cunning and cleverness of [c]unscrupulous men, [gamblers engaged] in every shifting form of trickery in inventing errors to mislead.*

15 *Rather, let our lives lovingly [d]express truth [in all things, speaking truly, dealing truly, living truly]. Enfolded in love, let us grow up in every way and in all things into Him Who is the Head, [even] Christ (the Messiah, the Anointed One).*

16 *For because of Him the whole body (the Church, in all its various parts), closely joined and firmly knit together by the joints and ligaments with which it is supplied, when each part [with power adapted to its need] is working properly [in all its functions], grows to full maturity, building itself up in love.*

Understanding the passage will prepare, you to have an open mind as being part of the body of Christ and unite with other believers and ministers for the Church to reach its full stature in Christ prepared to be the Glorious Church that Christ will meet on His Return.

CHAPTER 2

Living in a Dying World

With all the catastrophes, from terrorism to volcanic eruption, ash eruption, wars, a new epidemic outbreak of diseases, austerity measures and so on happening in the world today, have made many people confused, tired and hopeless about life. Due to this, the rate of Atheism is on the horizon. These days it seems these events are happening the more and faster.

In Matthew chapter 24, Jesus said, all these things will happen, but the end will not come until the

Gospel of the kingdom of God is preached to all nations. Now is the time to preach to the lost and confused souls. Sometimes churches and ministries focus so much on those within the walls of their jurisdiction and never reach or witness to those that are outside the Church. Our inability to not reach these group of people have made them loose hope in life, and many are turning to other religions that cannot save them or promise them any bright future. The worst of all is those who reject the existence of God, it's such a dangerous phenomenon, and such institutions are growing stronger and stronger every day.

After we become born again, we must share our new experience of salvation with others. Unfortunately, the Church herself does not encourage Evangelism because we are satisfied with the sheep we have in our care.

Now is the time to witness to the lost so that there will be more souls saved and fewer souls on their way to hell. Let us leave the ninety-nine saved sheep alone and go after the one lost sheep (Luke 15:4-7).

Jesus Parables of the Lost Sheep and the Lost Coin Luke 15:4-10

Parable of the lost Sheep Luke 15:4-7, Amplified Bible

4 What man of you, if he has a hundred sheep and should lose one of them, does not leave the ninety-nine in the wilderness (desert) and go after the hone that is lost until he finds it?

5 And when he has found it, he lays it on his [own] shoulders, rejoicing.

6 And when he gets home, he summons together [his] friends and [his] neighbors, saying to them, Rejoice with me, because I have found my sheep which was lost.

7 Thus, I tell you, there will be more joy in heaven over one [[c]especially] wicked person who repents ([d]changes his mind, abhorring his errors and misdeeds, and determines to enter upon a better course of life) than over ninety-nine righteous persons who have no need of repentance.

Summary of the Passage

Jesus spoke this parable to the Pharisees and scribes because they were complaining that He was welcoming sinners. He used the scenario of a shepherd who had a hundred sheepfold but lost one. Would he not go and look for the missing one and rejoice when he finds it? So is it when a sinner repents, turns from his wicked ways and comes into the true knowledge of salvation, heaven rejoices over one lost that has found Christ as His Saviour.

Parable of the lost Coin Luke 15:8-10, Amplified Bible

8 Or what woman, having ten [silver] drachmas [each one equal to a day's wages], if she loses one coin, does not light a lamp and sweep the house and look carefully and diligently until she finds it?

9 And when she has found it, she summons her [women] friends and neighbors, saying, Rejoice with me, for I have found the silver coin which I had lost.

10 Even so, I tell you, there is joy among and in the presence of the angels of God over one [[e]especially] wicked person who repents ([f]changes his mind for the better, heartily amending his ways, with abhorrence of his past sins).

Summary of the Passage

Jesus gave them another scenario of a woman who had ten silver pieces and lost one. Because all the coins are precious to her, she will make sure to look for the lost one until she finds it. And when she finds it, she will be very happy and call her friends to celebrate with her. Jesus explains this, as the same way heaven rejoices over a sinner who repents.

In a nutshell

As the body of Christ, we must not just be satisfied with the people we have in our congregation, we must go out and look for the lost souls and welcome them in our midst and then as we are rejoicing on earth the angels are rejoicing in heaven.

God wants all humanity to be saved and come into the true knowledge of His Son Jesus Christ. Therefore, we have a role to play to see that happen by going out and win souls for God's Kingdom. We must speak to the lost, the drunkards, the prostitutes, the people in a hopeless situation and so forth and tell them about the love of God, who sent His Son Jesus Christ to die for them so that they can have everlasting life, filled with purpose and a divine destiny.

CHAPTER 3
Evangelism Made Simple

What is the meaning of evangelism?

We will define the Word Evangelism and other words related to it, using the Oxford dictionaries.com definitions:

Evangelism

Evangelism is the spreading of the Christian Gospel by public preaching or personal witness.

Evangelise

Evangelise is to convert or seek to convert (someone) to Christianity.

Evangelist

An Evangelist is someone who seeks to convert others to the Christian faith, especially by public preaching.

According to Nelson's Bible dictionary, an Evangelist is a person authorised to proclaim the Gospel of Christ. In a narrow sense, the word refers to one of the gospel writers: Matthew, Mark, Luke, or John; however, the word means; "one who proclaims good tidings.

2 Timothy 4:5, Amplified Bible

As for you, be calm and cool and steady, accept and suffer unflinchingly every hardship, do the work of an evangelist, fully perform all the duties of your ministry.

From the definitions explained, we are going to look at Evangelism from 3 different perspectives:

1. Evangelism as a personal witness of the Christian faith

Evangelism as spreading the Christian Gospel by personal witness. As believers, we need to go about sharing the good news of salvation and convincing others of our Christian faith, through our day to day conversations and actions of love.

2. Evangelism as a local church goes out to Witness

Evangelism as spreading of the Christian Gospel by public preaching within a locality.

Sometimes we wait for people in our community to walk through our church doors, but in most cases, it does not happen that way, we need to go out and fetch in the harvest of souls.

3. Evangelism as in form of revivals or crusades

Evangelism as moving from place to place as being led by the Holy Spirit. The Evangelist in this category is also known as a missionary and is not attached to any specific locality or Church, and they move from place to place as the Holy Spirit leads them. Such people are gifted by God to walk in the office of an Evangelist. An Evangelist has a special anointing to be effective in winning souls in places where the Gospel has not yet reached. The Evangelist sets up the stage for crusades and brings in the Light of the good news to the people, by manifesting the Power of God through healing, signs, Wonders and preaching salvation. When people see the manifestation of God's power, it gives them hope in Christ, and many receive salvation. The Evangelist works with local churches in that locality so the new converts can be planted in churches and are continuously fed the Word of God and have fellowship with other believers. Those who walk in the office of an Evangelist have a special anointing to bring illumination of the Gospel through their preaching, because of this many receive hope and are in expectation of a bright future.

Understanding the various ways, we can evangelise; next, we are going to describe how each kind can be an effective witness of the good news of Christ.

We must also bear in mind that there are four categories of people that you will discover when you go out and witness.

Four Categories of People You will Encounter

Unbelievers: These are the category of people who have never heard the message of the Gospel being preached or did but never believed it.

Backsliders: These are the category of people, who once believed in the message but have strayed from the faith due to their lack of commitment. Some also have left the Church or

Christian faith due to an offence. They were offended by a church member or minister.

Lukewarm believers: These are the category of believers that have faith in God but lack the commitment to any local body. There are also those who go to Church once in a blue moon (occasionally). They go to Church on New Year's Eve, Resurrection weekend (Easter) or when there is a special occasion at church. Some also watch more of preaching on the television or online and refuse to be committed to a local Church, where they can be active, committed and fellowship with other believers. They think it is unnecessary.

Atheists or other Religions: The atheists are the hard nuts in this category; they don't believe that

God exists. There are other religions, but we know our Faith in Christ is the only way to the true living God.

We must always consider in which category the person belongs, to witness effectively to them. When we start a conversation, you can know what group they belong to. In this handbook, you will find scriptures about each category; This will give you guidelines on how to witness to each category of people effectively.

CHAPTER 4
Evangelism as a Personal Witness of the Christian Faith

How can I witness to lost souls?

As believers, the Lord will give you doors of opportunity to witness to people because of their problems and situations. Use those issues as an opportunity to talk about the love of God and the One who can solve any problem. Let them know that Jesus is the solution to all their problems. If it is a believer, remind them of what Jesus has already done for them on the cross, and His grace is enough to solve any problem they have.

Before we begin to witness to lost souls, we must First understand the meaning of repentance.

What is the meaning of Repentance?

Repentance means a turning away from sin, disobedience, or rebellion and a turning back to God. True repentance is godly sorrow for sin, an act of turning around and going in the opposite direction. This type of repentance leads to a fundamental change in a person's relationship with God.

Jesus began His ministry by preaching about Repentance.

Matthew 4:16-17, Amplified Bible

16 The people who sat (dwelt enveloped) in darkness have seen a great Light, and for those who sat in the land and shadow of death, Light has dawned.

17 From that time Jesus began to preach, crying out, Repent (change your mind for the better, heartily amend your ways, with abhorrence of your past sins), for the kingdom of heaven is at hand.

The people were in darkness until Jesus-the Light came and preached to them about repentance. You are the Light that Jesus is sending out into the darkness of people's lives to preach repentance to them so they can become the Light just as you are the Light.

Various Ways of Witnessing to Different Categories People

Witnessing to A Lost Soul

A lost soul is someone who has not heard the Good News of the Gospel or does not fully understand it. Such a person cannot live to the fullness of his life except He has received Jesus Christ as his Lord and Saviour.

How Can We Witness to a Lost Soul?

There are three steps we need to take when witnessing to a lost soul.

Step 1. Expressing God's love for humanity through His Son

As mentioned earlier, minister to them from the point of what problems or issues they are going through, shedding Light that there is hope in God and pray for them. After that, use the scripture below to explain God's love for humanity by sending His Son to die for our sins.

John 3:16-17

For God so loved the world that He gave His only begotten Son, that whoever believes in Him should not perish but have everlasting life. 17 For God did not send His Son into the world to condemn the world, but that the world through Him might be saved.

Step 2a. Confession of our Faith

Next step is to explain how important it is to make a verbal confession of what they believe, explain to them using, Romans 10:18-13 as reference.

Romans 10:8-13

---

8 But what does it say? "The word is near you, in your mouth and in your heart" (that is, the word of faith which we preach): 9 that if you confess with your mouth the Lord Jesus and believe in your heart that God has raised Him from the dead, you will be saved. 10 For with the heart one believes unto righteousness, and with the mouth, confession is made unto salvation. 11 For the scripture says, "Whoever believes on Him will not be put to shame." 12 For there is no distinction between Jew and Greek, for the same Lord over all is rich to all who call upon Him. 13 For "whoever calls on the name of the Lord shall be saved."

The scripture is explaining the importance of someone preaching about salvation. It goes on to explain that we can only be saved by first believing that Jesus died, and God resurrected Him from the dead. Our next step is to confess

Jesus Christ as our Lord and Saviour, meaning we have fully given Him control of our lives because he died for us.

 Ask the person to make a verbal confession that Jesus is Lord of their life by asking the following questions.

Step 2b. Answer the following questions:

1. Do you confess with your mouth that Jesus is Lord?

2. Do you believe in your heart, that God raised Jesus from the dead on the third day, after He died on the cross of Calvary?

3. Do you believe that Jesus can save you and turn your life around for good instead of the life you are living right now?

If they agree to all these statements and they believe in their heart what they have just said, THEY ARE SAVED!

Get them excited about it.

Step 3. Pray with such a person

Ask them to repeat this prayer after you or form a short similar prayer.

Lord, I thank you for forgiving me of my sins, saving my life from eternal destruction. I thank you for your Son whom you sent to die for my sins that I may live a good life in Christ.

I confess Jesus as my Lord and Saviour now and forever more in Jesus' Name, I pray. Amen

HURRAY, I AM SAVED!!!! I AM BORN AGAIN!!!

Let them know that heaven is rejoicing over their salvation and read the scripture to them.

Angels rejoice when a person repents.

Luke 15:10, Amplified Bible

10 Even so, I tell you, there is joy among and in the presence of the angels of God over one [especially] wicked person who repents (changes his mind for the better, heartily amending his ways, with abhorrence of his past sins).

3. Witnessing to backsliders or lukewarm Churchgoers

Step 1: Minister God's Word about Backsliding

God said He is married to the Backslider.

Jeremiah 3:14-15

"Return, O backsliding children," says the Lord; "for I am married to you. I will take you, one from a city and two from a family, and I will bring you to Zion. 15 And I will give you shepherds according to My heart, who will feed you with knowledge and understanding.

What is Backsliding?

Backsliding is the situation when somebody fails to do something that they agreed to do and returns to their former lousy behaviour.

A short message to a Backslider

If you went back to your old lifestyle He still loves you, all He wants you to do is to rededicate your life to Christ, and He will receive you with open arms, just as the father of the Prodigal Son received his Son when he came back home. Once you return, God will give you a Pastor/ shepherd that will feed you the right food of His Word for your spiritual growth.

Step 2: Use the Story of the Prodigal Son to explain God's love

Using the story of the Prodigal Son to minister to a backslider or a lukewarm churchgoer will express the love of God for them, even in their backslidden state. Many people who have backslidden believe they are not worthy of coming back to their faith in Christ, so they stop believing and growing in God. The story of the prodigal will heal them and give them hope to live again.

The story of the Prodigal Son (Luke 15:11-24)

11 Then He said: "A certain man had two sons.

12 "And the younger of them said to his father, 'Father, give me the portion of goods that falls to me.' So he divided to them his livelihood.

13 "And not many days after, the younger Son gathered all together, journeyed to a far country, and there wasted his possessions with prodigal living.

14 "But when he had spent all, there arose a severe famine in that land, and he began to be in want.

15 "Then he went and joined himself to a citizen of that country, and he sent him into his fields to feed swine.

16 "And he would gladly have filled his stomach with the pods that the swine ate, and no one gave him anything.

17 "But when he came to himself, he said, 'How many of my father's hired servants have bread enough and to spare, and I perish with hunger!

18 'I will arise and go to my father, and will say to him, "Father, I have sinned against heaven and before you,

19 "and I am no longer worthy to be called your Son. Make me like one of your hired servants." '

20 "And he arose and came to his father. But when he was still a great way off, his father saw him and had compassion, and ran and fell on his neck and kissed him.

---

21 *"And the son said to him, 'Father, I have sinned against heaven and in your sight, and am no longer worthy to be called your son.'*

22 *"But the father said to his servants, 'Bring out the best robe and put it on him and put a ring on his hand and sandals on his feet.*

23 *'And bring the fatted calf here and kill it, and let us eat and be merry;*

24 *'for this my son was dead and is alive again; he was lost and is found.' And they began to be merry.*

Summary of the passage

Let them know Jesus is waiting for them to come back home just like the Father of the Prodigal Son was waiting for his Son to come back home and when he did, he ran to meet him and celebrated him. Jesus is waiting for you to come back home and He will celebrate you and give you a chance to start a new life.

Step 3: Pray with such a person

Father, forgive me of all my sins and the way I have been living. Today I confess to living a new life in your Son Jesus Christ, I accept Him as my Lord and Saviour. Thank you for your unconditional love for me in Jesus name I pray. Amen.

Luke 15:10

10 "Likewise, I say to you, there is joy in the presence of the angels of God over one sinner who repents."

Just say this simple phrase to them with a big smile on your face.

"JESUS LOVES YOU" 😊

Step 4: Church attendance

Make sure they attend a living, Holy Spirit filled active church where they can grow in the Word of God and be active.

3. Witnessing To An Atheist

Step 1: Minister to them about God's creation of all things using the following scriptures.

Psalm 24:1

The earth is the Lord's, and all its fullness,

The world and those who dwell therein.

God owns the earth, He created all things and is in charge of all things including the people, the animals and everything that exists in it.

Psalm 14:1

The fool has said in his heart,

"There is no God."

They are corrupt,

They have done abominable works,

There is none who does good

A fool is a person who acts unwisely, silly or is deceptive. Only an unwise, silly or deceptive person will say there is no God.

These are hard nuts to crack because they don't even believe God exists. Just ask them questions around their existence and the natural elements such as, how trees grow, who feed the animals in the forest or the birds in the sky. Ask them questions aligning to human existence or reasoning, ask if they know the number of strands on their hair and quote the scripture that says God knows it. Give them the booklet to read about What am I doing on earth?

Luke 12:6-8

6 *"Are not five sparrows sold for two [a]copper coins? And not one of them is forgotten before God.* **7 But the very hairs of your Head are all numbered. Do not fear; therefore, you are of more value than many** *sparrows.*

Confess Christ Before Men

8 "Also I say to you, whoever confesses Me before men, him the Son of Man also will acknowledge before the angels of God.

Next Step

Follow the same steps we learned earlier on how to witness to a lost soul.

4. Evangelism as a local church goes out to witness

This type of Evangelism is the most unconsidered in the Church but the most effective way to win souls. Jesus said if we love one another, we are His true disciples.

If a church does not just talk about love to her members but steps out of the church premises and practice it to those in their communities, then we show that we are true Disciples of Christ. The local body Evangelism is the most effective and most exciting form of Evangelism. In the next chapter, we are going to give a detailed explanation of how we can be sent out to witness as a local body.

CHAPTER 5

Be Equipped to Be Sent Out

Every local body has been commissioned to go to all the world and preach to all nations and all people. Jesus commissioned His disciples to go into all the world and preach the Gospel. It is now time for us to go; this is the only way people will hear of the Good News. Therefore, it is crucial the local churches move out of their church walls and send out people to bring in the harvest of souls.

The Great Commission Mark 16:15-18

15 And He said to them, "Go into all the world and preach the Gospel to every creature. 16 He who believes and is baptised will be saved; but he who does not believe will be condemned. 17 And these signs will follow those who [d]believe: In My name they will cast out demons; they will speak with new tongues; 18 [e]they will take up serpents; and if they drink anything deadly, it will by no means hurt them; they will lay hands on the sick, and they will recover."

Summary of the Passage

Before Jesus went to heaven, He summoned His disciples and gave them a task. He asked them to go out into all the world and preach the Gospel; The Gospel is the good news, everyone who believes will also be empowered to become disciples and they also will lay hands on the sick and they shall be healed and so on. Which means when we preach the Gospel to others and they believe we are making disciples for our Lord Jesus Christ to do the same.

Be Equipped to Be Sent Out

Romans 10:14-15, Amplified Bible

14 But how are people to call upon Him whom they have not believed [in whom they have no faith, on whom they have no reliance]? And how are they to believe in Him [adhere to, trust in, and rely upon Him] of whom they have never heard? And how are they to hear without a preacher?

15 And how can men [be expected to] preach unless they are sent? As it is written, how beautiful are the feet of those who bring glad tidings! [How welcome is the coming of those who preach the good news of His good things!

For the people of the city to hear about the good news, the Church needs to prepare and equip the Evangelistic team and let them know they are going out under authority with instructions to follow, Just as we read from the scripture, they have to be sent to preach the good news. An example of such is in Matthew 10:1-15, when he sent out His twelve disciples.

Strategies for Evangelism as a Local Body

Step 1: These steps are guidelines, use them as need be or depending on the size of the Church or the Evangelism team.

The first step is to have a prayer solely focused on Evangelism, which includes the salvation of souls and believers having a passion to be sent out into the community and evangelise. When we have a focus, while we are praying, the Lord will give us names of streets and specific places to go.

The Intercessory prayer team, in conjunction with the Evangelism team, will first go out and pray on the streets where we intend to take over with the good news. Not more than a group of two to four people at a time.

Step 2: There will be four groups to go out. Each group prepared with similar scriptures of introducing the Gospel and inviting people to the Church. Each group will be given Bibles in the familiar language of that nation. For example, in Germany, we will take along with us German,

English and French Bibles. Handouts of the church vision and statement of beliefs, tracts, pictures for children with Jesus loves you written in different languages, they can also be colouring pictures. The group will need at least one person who speaks the primary language of the city or country.

NB: Before Introducing them to our Churches, we must first introduce them to the family of God by expressing God's love to all people and which our church is part of that family. We are One Body - One Family in Christ.

Strategies for Community Evangelism

Another way to Evangelise within the community is to have a stand or set up a stage outside the Church. This is called community evangelism

Community Evangelism is more effective as people on the streets will be inquisitive and would like to know what is going on.

Asking for Permission from local Authorities

It is essential to ask for permission from the local authority of your community. We need to be law abiding citizens; therefore, we must make sure we have a permit to do such an evangelism outreach within the community

Step 3: Feedback from Groups and follow ups

Each group will return with the feedback of the day and if possible, the names of people who decided to give their life to Christ or to come to Church. If they encounter any difficulty, we need to know. Also, if there is anyone who is severely sick or in need, we need to know and find ways in which we can go back and help. There Must always be a follow up.

NB: Helping or visiting people must not be based on them coming to our churches or receiving salvation; it Must be based on the Love of God towards all people. The only way we can win souls is by expressing the Love of God without being biased of race, gender, colour, religion or denomination.

Volunteers

During the time the groups are on the street evangelising, we still need people who will pray at the Church and worship as the Evangelism team go forth. We will also need volunteers who will take care of the children and supply food for the day.

Interpreters

Apart from adults who speak the local language of the community, children who speak the language of the country could also be interpreters. All they need to do is to get used to the scriptures that will be used for that day.

Evangelism class

The church must prepare the minds of the people by organising an Evangelism class for all participants. It is also important that the interpreters must understand and learn the scriptures both adults and young children.

For street Evangelism, we could also have entertainment for the children.

These are the following teams to consider for Effective Evangelism

Evangelism

Praise and Worship

Intercessory prayer

Childcare

Hospitality

Materials that need to be available

1.Bibles in various languages

2. Vision statement.

3. Tracts in multiple languages.

4. Happy pictures and colouring for children.

Hospitality

The Church can provide, the food for the people and needs for the children or voluntarily donations can be made by all.

Suggested day

Must be agreed upon by all leaders involved.

Local Churches Coming Together for The Sake Of Evangelism

A group of local churches can also come together and have an evangelism outreach for their community: This is a platform to win more souls and an excellent opportunity to see local churches work together, this attracts a greater blessing of God upon His church. Though we might bear different names or different denominations, we are One body in Christ, One Lord and One Spirit of God in us all.

We can still follow all the above guidelines and make adjustments where need be. It might only take more time and resources to prepare such an Outreach.

When the people in our communities see such a commitment of local churches coming together, it will attract them to want to be be part of us; This is the expression of true discipleship and the love of God for all mankind. Then that gives them a reason to believe in our God.

When we are unified as the body of Christ, it attracts the blessings of God upon His people. Though we might bear different names or different denominations, but we are One body in Christ, One Lord and One Spirit of God in us all.

In conclusion

Every believer can be a witness for Christ if they understand these simple guidelines and explanations in this handbook.

Also, Churches regardless of their names or denominations came come together and have an Evangelism Outreach project for the community, since we all make up the One Body of Christ.

Please send us an email if you have any questions or you need us to format tracts for your ministry or community Evangelism Outreach Project.

You can also email us for large quantities of this book.

Email: info@glorypublishers.org

Check our website for our course on Evangelism

Course Title:

EVANGELISM IN THE 21ST CENTURY

WEBSITE: www.glorypublishers.org

ABOUT THE AUTHOR

Yinka Oloyede is an end time messenger of God, who, through her ministry, has a passion for preparing the body of Christ for His second coming and inviting those who are lost to receive Jesus Christ as their Lord and Saviour, so they can also be in expectation of His coming.

She introduces herself as one called by God and ordained by God to be a messenger of Hope, Peace and Love to the nations of the world through the CALL TO PRAY, INTERCEDE, ACT AND THROUGH HER GIFT OF WRITNG.

She also has a Passion for the youth, teaching them to be Kingdom Builders and preparing them for the second coming of Christ.

Yinka is a mother, blessed with four active children, Yetunde, Tobi, Femi and Bunmi. They reside in Germany.

She is also the author of 'The Power of Intercession and its Study Guide;' 'The Birthing of a Glorious Church and its Study Workbook,' 'God speaks to the Unknown Prayer Journal and God Speaks to me Prayer Journal notebook,' and the 'Baptism of the Holy Spirit with the Evidence of speaking in Tongues.'

All her books are available at

www.glorypublishers.org

THE
POWER
OF
INTERCESSION
YINKA OLOYEDE

STUDY GUIDE
THE
POWER
OF
INTERCESSION
YINKA OLOYEDE

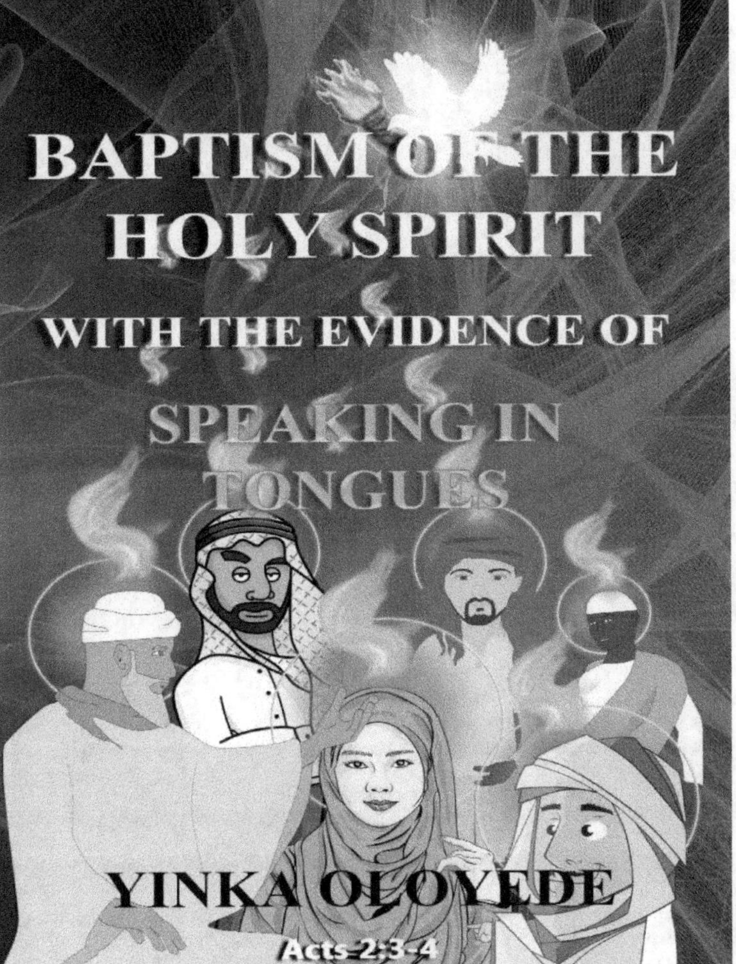

BAPTISM OF THE HOLY SPIRIT
WITH THE EVIDENCE OF
SPEAKING IN TONGUES
YINKA OLOYEDE
Acts 2:3-4

GOD SPEAKS
To the Unknown

Prayer Journal

How to Maintain a Meaningful
and Productive Prayer Journal

Yinka Oloyede

GOD SPEAKS TO ME

Journal notebook

YINKA OLOYEDE

www.ingramcontent.com/pod-product-compliance
Lightning Source LLC
LaVergne TN
LVHW011603210726
843509LV00016BA/830